A Director's Gu

G000253167

Management buy-outs

GUIDING DIRECTORS THROUGH THE CRITICAL FACTORS OF THE MANAGEMENT BUY-OUT PROCESS

Editor, Director Publications: Tom Nash
Managing Editor: Lesley Shutte
Production Manager: Victoria Davies
Commercial Director: Simon Seward
Design: Halo Design
Chairman: George Cox
Managing Director: Andrew Main Wilson

Published for the Institute of Directors and Phildrew Ventures
by Director Publications Ltd
116 Pall Mall London SW1Y 5ED

Editorial: 020 7766 8910
Sponsorship: 020 7766 8885
Production: 020 7766 8960
Copy sales: 020 7766 8766
Facsimile: 020 7766 8990

Price £9.95

YOURS TO HAVE AND TO HOLD
BUT NOT TO COPY

Director Publications Ltd
116 Pall Mall
London SW1Y 5ED

Kogan Page Ltd
120 Pentonville Road
London N1 9JN

© Director Publications 1999

British Library Cataloguing in Publication Data
A CIP record for this book is available from the British Library
ISBN 0 7494 3247 0

Printed and bound in Great Britain

Contents

Time for a change of direction?

Creative Capital for Management Buy-Outs

If you've got an uneasy feeling that your company took a wrong turn somewhere, it's probably time to talk to Phildrew Ventures.

We specialise in Management Buy Outs or Buy Ins anywhere between £20 million and £200 million and tend to attract management teams who have a bold new vision for their enterprise.

In us, they find a partner who can not only provide the necessary capital, but also one with the imagination to share that vision, backed by the experience and stamina to see it through.

So if it's time your company changed drivers, it's time to call Phildrew Ventures.

Phildrew Ventures

Phildrew Ventures, 100 Liverpool Street,
London EC2M 2RH. Tel: 020 7568 9000
e-mail: phildrewventures@ubs.com
Phildrew Ventures is regulated by IMRO

A MEMBER OF UBS CAPITAL,
THE PRIVATE EQUITY DIVISION OF UBS AG.

Risks and rewards

George Cox, Director General, Institute of Directors

The numerous successful management buy-outs of recent years have released the entrepreneurial energies of many UK managers and have played an important role in creating an enterprise culture.

Typically, directors taking part in an MBO have been employed by large organisations throughout their careers. Their motives often include a desire to "run their own show", without the corporate shackles imposed by a parent company. An MBO offers a chance to prove themselves – and, of course, to make some serious money.

But to go through an MBO can be tough and fraught with risks. The stakes are high and, invariably, the deal involves months of difficult negotiations. There are new relationships to be forged with professional advisers, equity investors and banks, and a mass of documentation to cope with. Directors may struggle to raise the personal finance necessary – and there can be a heavy toll on personal life.

There may be times when they doubt whether the deal will ever happen – or if it is worth the pain involved. But for those who are up to the challenge of an MBO, it can be the high point of their careers.

The key elements of a successful buy-out are realism, careful planning, commitment, hard work and good advice. Above all, any director who is contemplating participation in a buy-out must learn fast, wherever possible drawing on the experience of others who have gone down the same path. This Guide covers the major factors involved and will prove an indispensable aid.

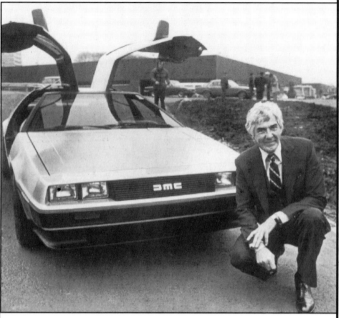

Time for a different approach?

The evolving buy-out market

Richard Northedge, Deputy Editor, Sunday Business

Suddenly management buy-outs have become the solution to the small company problem: private equity funds are happily picking up the companies that the stockmarket has abandoned.

Ironically, in many instances the same fund managers who regard the companies as too small to be worth dealing in on the Stock Exchange, and who thus contribute to the poor liquidity that forces directors to abandon the quoted sector, are exactly the same institutions that are now eagerly backing buy-outs of those same companies.

Public-to-private deals have become the hot trend. There were 27 in 1998 and their value rose eightfold to £2.7bn, but those totals had already been exceeded by the middle of 1999 as more directors, disillusioned with the disadvantages of a share listing, chose to gear up on cheap money and revitalise their equity interest by retreating into the private sector again. Private equity funds have record funds – more than £12bn – to finance the trend, much of it pouring over from the US.

Venture capital investments ultimately need an exit and flotation has proved almost impossible recently. But markets turn and eventually small company flotations will be back in favour.

Will the directors who are currently so keen to spurn a share listing return to the market? Perhaps. When the venture capitalists want their exit, they may well look to large corporations and try to arrange a trade sale – or they may replace the existing management with new directors who have not been scarred by the quoted experience. There seems ample scope for institutions to finance a buy-out of the buy-out.

Time for a change of leadership?

Creative Capital for Management Buy-Outs

Death or glory might be a justifiable rallying cry in battle, but it's a highly questionable one in business.

If you feel your company is pitching its tents in the wrong place, it's time to talk to Phildrew Ventures about an MBO or MBI.

We generally look at ventures between £20 million and £200 million.

But our contribution goes further than just capital. We also provide advice and support based on long experience, backed by the willingness, imagination and stamina to look beyond the easy deal.

So if it's time you made a stand of your own, it's time to call Phildrew Ventures.

Phildrew Ventures

Phildrew Ventures, 100 Liverpool Street,
London EC2M 2RH. Tel: 020 7568 9000
e-mail: phildrewventures@ubs.com
Phildrew Ventures is regulated by IMRO

A MEMBER OF UBS CAPITAL,
THE PRIVATE EQUITY DIVISION OF UBS AG.

Chapter 1

Today's buy-out market

Professor Mike Wright (director), Dr Mark Albrighton (research associate) and Andrew Burrows (researcher) of CMBOR, the Centre for Management Buy-Out Research at University of Nottingham Business School, report on the current status of the UK buy-out industry

In 1998 the total value of buy-outs and buy-ins in the UK reached a record level for the third successive year, increasing by 35 per cent to £14.2bn. A major factor was the rise in average transaction value from £15m to £21m. From a 1997 peak of 692, total volume eased to 670 – still the second highest level ever.

Boom conditions built up during 1998 and in the final quarter economic uncertainty led financiers to reconsider their position. Depressed market conditions continued into the first quarter of 1999, but the second quarter saw a marked recovery. As fears of recession receded, total market value rose 30 per cent on the first quarter to £3.8bn. However, activity volume failed to recover during the second quarter as confidence was slow to revive and deals took longer to complete.

BUY-OUT TYPES

Rapid market growth up to mid-1998 was driven largely by the re-emergence of externally initiated transactions. While these have traditionally been management buy-ins (MBIs), in recent years two other forms have developed: the hybrid management buy-in /buy-out (BIMBO) and the investor – or institutional – buy-out (IBO). Buy-ins (including BIMBOs and IBOs) strengthened their deal value position in 1998 to £9.1bn – a record 64 per cent of the market. BIMBOs developed in response to the poor record of buy-ins completed in the late 1980s, when receivership rates of about a third necessitated major re-assessment. A tendency to overpay for acquisitions led to relatively high gearing unable to withstand the recessionary period. Another major factor was the failure of venture capitalists and new external management teams to identify problem areas during due diligence. Completing a deal jointly with selected internal management could reduce such risks significantly.

The development of the IBO market over the last year has been spectacular. CMBOR recorded transactions worth £6bn in 1998. In a typical IBO, a venture capitalist is asked to engage in an auction for a large divestment transaction. This process may be conducted directly by the vendor or, more typically, through an intermediary. The venture capitalist may not have direct access to management until it becomes a short-listed bidder or later, so may have to consider head-hunting a new CEO or even managing the company itself.

Larger companies have more sophisticated accounting and financial systems than smaller buy-ins, but problems can still emerge in due diligence, especially given the time constraints of analysing businesses with an international operating structure. Also, auction-inspired competition may result in overpayment.

VENDOR AND VENTURE CAPITALIST CONSIDERATIONS

The increase of IBOs reflects both vendor and venture capitalist considerations. For the vendor, increasing emphasis on shareholder value has encouraged auctions. Major divestors are well aware of venture capitalists' interest in acquisitions. In larger divestments, vendors may fear failure to maximise the sale price if management become closely involved too early, especially if considering their own buy-out transaction.

Venture capitalists have been highly successful in raising funds and now have to invest these prudently while being seen to complete deals. These factors increase willingness to participate in auctions. Venture capitalists are also now more proactive in seeking market niches and identifying potential transactions ahead of rivals.

DEAL SOURCES

Another development in the MBO market is the re-emergence of deals involving quoted companies that later de-list ("public-to-private"). Public-to-private deals accounted for almost a fifth of total buy-out market value in 1998, when 27 such buy-outs were completed, more than double the previous record. In the first half of 1999, 21 deals were completed, with another 11 announced but not unconditional.

Recent going-private deals have typically involved small to medium-sized companies of little interest to large institutional investors and suffering a lack of share liquidity – some operating in unfashionable sectors, or experiencing problems but having potential through restructuring.

In the first half of 1999 this pattern changed: larger transactions were completed (including six valued above £100m) and competing bids by financial buyers began to emerge, with public-to-private deals representing almost a third of market value. There are signs that institutional investors feel management should be increasing value for existing shareholders rather than seeking buy-outs, but the question remains as to why they appear reluctant to recognise value in smaller stocks.

There has also been a significant increase in purchases from private owners (including secondary buy-outs from venture capitalists). In 1998 these accounted for almost half of all MBOs (a record) and almost three-fifths of MBIs.

Another recent market feature is the development of leveraged build-ups and the emergence of serial entrepreneurs. Leveraged build-ups involve creating a group of companies based on an initial buy-out, to which further major acquisitions are added. For private equity backers, these may offer a means of achieving higher returns to offset increasing entry prices.

Such transactions are attractive where a strong medium-sized platform investment forms the base for rationalising a fragmented industry. Good management is needed to identify and integrate a stream of acquisitions while maintaining operational activities.

EXITS

1996 marked a record level of buy-out and buy-in investment realisations (201), but exits fell to 183 in 1998. Trade sales appear to be slowing down in 1999, and flotations have been adversely affected by institutional investors disregarding smaller stocks. This mirror image of the rationale for increased public-to-private deals saw buy-out/buy-in flotations fall from 41 in 1996 to 14 in 1998. In the first half of 1999 only three buy-outs and buy-ins came to market, with the presence of an IT element influencing market attractiveness.

In contrast, secondary buy-outs have increased six-fold since 1991, to 49 in 1998. In these transactions the original buy-out is refinanced with a new ownership structure. The original venture capitalist backer exits and sometimes a second-tier or external management team takes over.

The growth of secondary buy-outs may mark a recognition by private equity providers of the validity of buying from another private equity player, especially where the vendor needs to sell because it is a closed-end fund nearing maturity. Around 250 secondary buy-outs/buy-ins have now been completed, triggered by various factors – for example, management resisting alternative exit plans proposed by the venture capitalist because of a long-term desire to remain independent, but needing additional funding for a major expansion. The number of buy-outs and buy-ins going into receivership declined steadily from a 1991 peak of 120 to 51 in 1997. 1998's economic slowdown caused this level to rise, but in 1999 receiverships have again eased off.

DEAL STRUCTURING

In smaller transactions (below £10m), although average equity levels fell in 1998 to their lowest this decade at 31 per cent of total deal financing, average managerial equity stakes rose to 66 per cent, their highest for six years. In larger deals average managerial equity stakes fell to a 1990s low of 26 per cent, reflecting the increase in institutionally driven deals and higher prices being paid to vendors.

Financial structuring has been affected by the considerable liquidity of most fund suppliers and competition for transaction mandates. Debt financing innovations and new market entrants have also had an impact. Two important debt-related developments are the emergence of alphabet loans and the use of the European high-yield bond market to fund larger buy-outs. There is an availability in the market of a continuum of debt instruments allowing investors and issuers to identify the different risk–return layers in individual deals and to match companies' cashflow profiles with repayment profiles.

These relatively recent developments have helped lift the share of debt in buy-out financing. The average share of senior debt in larger deals rose to almost 50 per cent in 1998. The level of mezzanine within these deals increased significantly to its highest share of financings since 1992. The total mezzanine involved in buy-outs completed in 1998 was £2.07bn – £1.63bn of debt rated at BBB and below (12 deals) and £0.44bn of privately placed mezzanine (52 deals).

ALPHABET LOANS

The alphabet loan market can enable buy-out financiers to minimise the costs and loss of flexibility associated with subordinated debt. Alphabet loans involve senior term loans in structured layers. Where there is a need to restructure, it may be preferable to delay capital repayments to retain cashflow inside the MBO company. Instruments may be used that either have a one-year or two-year repayment holiday and/or are only repayable in one payment when the company is sold or floated at a pre-determined date.

In larger transactions where it is viable for debt providers to separate these instruments, more than one layer of senior debt may be provided. In these cases the A loan typically has a seven-year life; B and, if applicable, C loans generally have longer maturity and nominal amortisation prior to A loan repayment, carrying higher rates of interest. These debt layers have equal priority in the event of default.

HIGH-YIELD BONDS

The high-yield debt market for buy-outs in the UK and Europe began developing significantly from 1997 into the first half of 1998. World stock-market turmoil mid-year effectively brought the market to a halt until early 1999. This response to changing macroeconomic factors contributed to a timely re-evaluation of the market after entry prices rose sharply and measures of the ability of buy-outs to service debt deteriorated. After a quietish first quarter, the European high-yield debt market saw issues totalling around $3bn in April/May 1999.

Overall, the distinction between alphabet and high-yield debt has blurred as financiers have issued both high-yield bonds and long-term securitisations, often with similar ratings. A number of buy-outs have now issued investment grade rated bonds. As a result, debt structures in buy-outs are markedly more fluid.

OUTLOOK

The UK environment that has enabled the buy-out industry to flourish – managers' increasing entrepreneurship and desire to own equity, established corporate restructuring processes, good networks of financiers and other intermediaries, investors' ability to make gains – remains firmly in place.

Following significant fundraising, entry into the market by US players and the development of new debt-based financing instruments, substantial funds are available for investment in buy-outs. Economic and financial indicators have enabled the buy-out market to develop over the last few years, resulting in greater stability. Now that fears of recession have receded, the market looks set for further strong growth as significant-sized deals reappear. However, there is a continuing need for prudence in the pricing and structuring of higher-value transactions in particular.

CMBOR, the Centre for Management Buy-Out Research at University of Nottingham Business School is sponsored by Barclays Private Equity and Deloitte & Touche.

Chapter 2

A tale of two buy-outs

Business writer Guy Dresser focuses on two companies that successfully came through the buy-out process. Despite operating in very different sectors and envisaging contrasting exit routes, the businesses displayed common factors that favoured a positive outcome

Small public companies have again emerged as a major source of buy-outs, ten years after the 1980s MBO boom, when a flood of businesses took the public-to-private route. This time it's primarily the City's disregard for these small cap companies that's prompting them to take the plunge. In institutional investors' eyes, any business worth less than £100m is of peripheral interest only.

These are companies whose shares have fallen out of favour, trading on such low p/e ratios that it is extremely hard for them to raise equity funding for the acquisitions that would get them to as size at which they could be taken seriously. Thus they miss out on exciting acquisition opportunities that crop up, and get left behind by rivals who are better placed to fund them: a classic "Catch 22" situation.

THE PLIGHT OF THE SMALL PLC

Harrington Food Group (formerly JLI), a food processing company turning over £65m a year, took the public-to-private route in February 1998. Changing public tastes had caused one of its subsidiaries, a packaged nuts supplier, to run into difficulties. Snack-eaters were warming to newer, rival snacks like tortilla chips and extruded products such as Quavers and Wotsits.

The Leeds-based subsidiary, Tee Gee Snacks, was eventually closed, but exceptional costs and write-offs of £9.9m took their toll.

By 1997 shareholders' funds had almost halved from £28m to £15m and, unsurprisingly, some major investors wanted to cut their losses.

A BIG PLC OPPORTUNITY

The second major source of buy-outs is the restructuring undertaken by large PLCs intent on following the City's maxim that focus is everything. Directors of subsidiaries deemed not to have a long-term future within the overall business become frustrated when they realise that the board's attention is focused elsewhere in the group. Left to their own devices, they are often starved of the funds they need in order to develop. Such businesses can begin to wither on the vine and perform less well than they would under more dedicated owners who understood them better.

The directors of Dowty's electronics division felt just such frustration. Focusing on aircraft and engine controls, maritime anti-submarine warfare and avionics systems, the division consisted of seven principal businesses – all acquired by TI in 1992 as part of its £510m takeover of Dowty.

Dowty itself had tried, unsuccessfully, to sell the electronics division before it was swallowed up. TI, having bought Dowty for its aerospace expertise, now made it clear that the electronics businesses were considered non-core, and ran them accordingly.

Dr Julian Blogh, then managing director of Dowty Avionics, spotted an opportunity. However, he faced opposition from TI's board, which declared that it would not sell the businesses to the existing directors. Blogh therefore resigned, and began the long drawn-out process of buying the business with institutional support. For this purpose he hired Arthur Andersen, auditors to Dowty before its acquisition, who steered him through the process of appointing bankers, lawyers and venture capitalists – Phildrew Ventures and Montagu Private Equity.

Negotiations dragged on, complicated by the involvement of two venture capital firms and a consortium of banks led by the Bank of Scotland. The £40m deal, concluded more than six months later in October 1993, resulted in the successful formation of Ultra

Electronics, which has bloomed under new ownership. In the nine months to the end of 1992 the seven businesses had made aggregate pre-tax profits of some £4.8m. As Ultra grew fast under its new management, pre-tax profits quadrupled to £21.06m in 1998 on revenues of £158.6m, almost double the 1993 figure of about £88m.

Ultra went on to float on the stock market in October 1996 for £162.5m, rose rapidly to £175m and by mid-1999 was capitalised at £270m. It remains Phildrew's most successful investment to date.

COMMON FACTORS

Despite operating in distinct industries and being the subject of deals that were structured differently, Harrington Food Group and Ultra share many of the characteristics essential for a successful MBO.

Both had a strong position in a niche market that presented fearsome barriers to entry for would-be rivals. Food might be a low-margin, high-competition business, but Harrington operates in particular niches. Its activities include the supply of popcorn to most UK cinema chains and the provision of tons of frozen herbs to food manufacturers for speciality breads, chilled soups and ready-made meals. Ultra, meanwhile, is a high-tech player in a highly specialist field, providing submarine detection sonobuoys, aircraft computers, and command and control systems, including those found on the Challenger II tank and Eurofighter.

At both Ultra and Harrington Food Group the directors thought they could run the business better under their own steam. In each case they formulated a business plan envisaging strong post-buy-out growth, convincing venture capitalists that they were capable of achieving the forecast level of return. Again in both cases there was a desire by the current owners to offload the businesses, making a deal more likely.

THE IMPORTANCE OF THE EXIT STRATEGY

The two companies' directors were also clearly focused on their exit strategy – an essential factor in obtaining venture capital support.

Blogh says flotation was always the most likely exit route

for Ultra: "We are quite a diverse business and no one trade buyer would have wanted to acquire everything. The effort involved in selling the group bit by bit would not have been worthwhile."

For Harrington Food Groups' chief executive Tony Orvis, however, a stock market flotation is not on the cards. Appointed chief executive in 1997 following a boardroom re-shuffle, he says this was clear from the start. Few of the circumstances that led JLI off the market in the first place have changed, so the idea of growing into a diversified food conglomerate and relisting at some stage in the future is a non-starter. Harrington will eventually be sold off via a series of trade sales.

Now away from the stock market, with its board able to improve the business without worrying about the share price or being obliged to deliver improved profit figures every six months, Harrington is on course. Its first post-MBO disposal has already taken place. Birmingham-based Cadec, a nut processor for the industrial sector, was sold in December 1998, eleven months after the £45m buy-out – again backed by Phildrew Ventures.

STRAINS OF THE MBO PROCESS

However, the bid processes themselves turned out to be very different experiences for Ultra Electronics and Harrington Food Group. For Blogh the buy-out process proved fraught and highly stressful, not least because his resignation meant that he had no income. The longer the process dragged on, the more he ate into his resources. And, to cap it all, he worked mostly from home, only just coping with the lack of administrative back-up he was used to.

Having circumvented TI's opposition to selling him the business, Blogh nevertheless found the group a difficult negotiating partner. Securing exclusivity proved a major challenge, with TI threatening to sell the businesses to a third party if it didn't get what it wanted.

The urgency of the situation was compounded by the recession, which meant that many banks were unwilling to extend their exposure in the aerospace sector. Although Ultra's military work consisted of major long-term contracts with the British and overseas governments, the civil aerospace industry was in the downward part of the cycle and business confidence was at a record low.

It was not a good time to be raising money to invest in the sector, Blogh recalls: "The Bank of Scotland did well to hold together a consortium of six banks to back the buy-out, but on two separate occasions the finances fell through after first one and then another bank pulled out."

Six years have done little to dull the memory of the emotions Blogh felt as the buy-out teetered on the brink of collapse. "There were several times in the whole process when I seriously questioned whether the buy-out could be achieved," he admits.

"It proved to be six months of day-to-day talks, first with the venture capitalists, then TI and then the banks. There were so many people involved and all needed to be kept informed and negotiated with. The sense of relief when it was all over was enormous. By comparison, the flotation was a doddle."

KEEPING A COOL HEAD

For Tony Orvis, however, the management buy-out process holds few unpleasant memories. This is something he attributes to his financial advisers, Campbell Lutyens.

"Our financial advisers were crucial. For most people it's your first experience of doing a buy-out, so it was important to have a firm that has handled previous public-to-private transactions. We also knew we didn't want a large firm where we'd be the responsibility of a team of newly qualified graduates. Most of all we got on at a personal level, and that's important whoever you're appointing.

"The one lesson I learned was to be objective. Don't get emotional but challenge yourself. Keep asking what would happen if the worst-case scenario happened. By spending a very long time on the business plan we were sure of our ground when we went to present our case to the venture capitalists."

Time to take over?

Creative Capital for Management Buy-Outs

All companies have captains. But sometimes even the best of captains outstay their welcome.

Which is when the rest of the crew starts thinking MBO or MBI - and where Phildrew Ventures comes in.

As you'd expect, the principal way we can help is with capital: we tend to look at ventures between £20 million and £200 million.

But just as important, we provide advice and support based on long experience, backed by the willingness and imagination to look beyond the easy deal.

So if it's time for new hands at the helm, it's time to call Phildrew.

Phildrew Ventures

Phildrew Ventures, 100 Liverpool Street,
London EC2M 2RH. Tel: 020 7568 9000
e-mail: phildrewventures@ubs.com

Phildrew Ventures is regulated by IMRO

**A MEMBER OF UBS CAPITAL,
THE PRIVATE EQUITY DIVISION OF UBS AG.**

Chapter 3

Choosing a venture capital partner

Frank Neale, partner at Phildrew Ventures, emphasises that the success of a deal depends on the quality of the partnership

Before you set out to find a venture capital partner, it is vital to understand the true nature of venture capital. Venture capital is all about a business partnership based on equity investment. In a management buy-out transaction the venture capitalist takes on numerous roles, in particular:

- *Identifying potential opportunities;*

- *Evaluating targets to ensure an MBO would work;*

- *Negotiating the deal with the vendor;*

- *Arranging the finance;*

- *Undertaking due diligence;*

- *Managing the whole process to ensure a deal takes place;*

- *Post-investment support and monitoring;*

- *Handling the approach to the exit.*

KEY CRITERIA

Before you actually make the decision on a particular venture capitalist, it is helpful if you set down the criteria upon which you are going to base your judgement.

When you are researching venture capitalists and meeting them, you can develop your questioning around these criteria.

The factors you should consider include:

■ *Financial objectives;*

■ *Size of transaction;*

■ *Funds available;*

■ *Type of deal;*

■ *Sector experience;*

■ *Geographic location;*

■ *Method of decision making;*

■ *Post-investment relationships;*

■ *Integrity.*

It is clearly imperative if you are entering a business partnership that you have compatible financial objectives – most, but not all, venture capitalists will be looking to make a capital gain on their investment in the medium term (say five years).

Examine your own financial objectives carefully and find a compatible partner – don't just parrot: "We are looking for a flotation in three years," if you don't really mean it. It will only lead to grief at a later stage and is largely unnecessary as there are sources of capital with longer-term objectives.

Attitudes to dividends vary widely and should be tested. An obvious question to ask, but often forgotten, is: "Does the venture capitalist have the funds available to support your deal not only now, but also in the future?" This will obviously be of much greater importance if acquisitions are a key ingredient of your strategy. If the venture capitalist has specific sector experience, so much the better as he will be familiar with your industry issues and terminology.

Another factor often overlooked by people seeking venture capital is the method of decision making and the relationships post-investment. As a director, you will be used to making quick decisions - make sure your venture capital partner can keep pace with you. Also, explore how he is going to get involved post-acquisition - do you want support? Is the venture capitalist capable of giving it? Some venture capitalists like to take a major role as the business moves forward, but most will settle for a non-executive directorship - but it is still worth your while making sure he is going to be value for money. Check out who will take up the non-executive directorship, as this will be the focal point of your longer term relationship.

Perhaps of greatest importance in the end is business and personal integrity. When you embark on an MBO you will be confident that everything in your business plan will work out reasonably well. Of course, in reality the venture capitalist knows (or he should do!) that things will go wrong from time to time. When they do, you need to be sure that you have chosen a partner who will play fair when things don't go quite according to plan.

FINDING YOUR VENTURE CAPITAL PARTNER

Personal recommendation is usually the best way of finding any new supplier and venture capital is no different. As around 5,000 MBOs have been completed in the UK in the last ten years, there is likely to be a business in your town that has been through the process. Track one down and gain from its experience.

Your accountant or lawyer will also almost certainly have experience and should be consulted at an early stage for guidance on who might be the appropriate backer for your deal. If you are not satisfied with, or are unable to use personal recommendations, there are a number of directories that can help. The British Venture Capital Association (BVCA) Directory of Members is the best one to start with, as it gives you a brief profile of each firm and what it is looking for.

For much smaller transactions the BVCA also publishes a *Directory of Business Angels*, that specialise at the smaller end of the spectrum - less than £500,000. The BVCA is at: Essex House, 12-13 Essex Street, London, WC2R 3AA, telephone: 020-7240 3846.

CASE STUDY

As someone who had never attempted a management buy-out before, Tony Orvis relied on his financial advisers, Campbell Lutyens, to help identify potential venture capital backers for his bid.

Campbell Lutyens drew up a long list of potential equity backers, which was narrowed down after discussions as to what exactly the management team was looking for.

"Campbell Lutyens had already dealt with many on the list and knew what types of deal they would back," explains Orvis. "Our advisers made the first approaches, then we went to see half a dozen potential backers."

Orvis claims that many venture capitalists will say they are seriously interested in a company simply as a means of having the chance to turn it down if they discover it is not to their taste. Some venture capitalists won't back deals below a certain size. Others restrict themselves to a certain number of core industry areas.

"The whole exercise was very interesting. The venture capital firms were quite different, much more so than I expected. Some were formal and bureaucratic, others were easier to get along with.

"We expected to have vigorous debates about what management's share of the business would be. But in the first instance we had to weed the list from six to two." In the end it came down to how serious firms were about backing a public-to-private bid.

"Lots of them said they were seriously interested in public-to-privates, but when it came to the crunch they weren't really," says Orvis. "The final decider for us was the rapport we struck up with Phildrew Ventures. Many things about them could be said of other firms, but it's the small things that make the difference. You can't understate the importance of the personal relationship. You'll have to work with them for years, through good times and bad, so you have to have mutual respect and an ability to work together well.

MAKING THE APPROACH

If you are thinking of an MBO, before approaching the venture capitalist you must check your legal situation. Ideally, you should have formal board authority before speaking to venture capitalists, but if this is not appropriate then ensure that you do not breach any fiduciary responsibilities.

You will need a concise business plan and summary. Make a brief telephone call to the venture capitalist to check he is interested in your type of proposal and then send him the summary. Whatever you do, don't scatter business plans around like confetti. Aim to see three or four venture capital groups who have expressed genuine interest in your plan.

MEETING THE VENTURE CAPITALIST

When you get an appointment with a venture capitalist try and get him to your site if you can, as you will feel more comfortable and he will gain a better impression of your business. Unfortunately, he'll probably insist on the first meeting being at his offices as it is a more economical use of his time.

As time will be very limited – plan on no longer than an hour – and you are likely to get only one chance, make sure you present your business in the best light. Have a good summary of the key points and be on top of the numbers.

If possible, make sure the key members of the team are with you. The venture capitalist will spend most of the meeting quizzing you on your business, but do try and keep back a little time so you can ask him some questions. Ask for a written proposal and ask for some references so you can talk to other chief executives the firm has worked with. The venture capitalist will be doing lots of due diligence on you, so don't forget to do some on him.

TAKING THE DECISION

If you are running a business of any size and strength you will by now have several proposals from a number of credible venture capitalists, all of which meet your initial decision-making criteria. So how do you choose? At this stage it is worth recalling the opening paragraph and remembering that you are on the verge of a new long-term business relationship.

This whole process is a little like marriage – you've been to the disco, eyed up all the potential partners and its time to enter the courtship phase. It comes down, therefore, to how comfortable you feel with individuals and the relationships you are likely to form with them. But don't lose sight of the real objectives, which are to buy the company and make it a successful investment for all concerned.

THE FIRST STEPS OF THE ENGAGEMENT

Once you have decided which venture capitalist to work with, make sure you are clear about who is doing what in the few weeks prior to the marriage ceremony.

There are many tasks to be completed – appointing a bank or two, taking personal financial advice, taking insurance advice, pensions advice, property advice, legal advice and accounting advice – to name but a few.

There will be many advisers vying for your attention – if only to justify the high level of fees they are going to invoice you for soon after completion – and if you are not careful some may well stray into the territory of others. It is important, therefore, to be absolutely clear with your venture capital partner at the outset about who is leading the transaction. Agree a timetable with him, a list of tasks, key responsibilities and a critical path.

Now you've found your venture capital partner, the real fun of courting can begin.

Chapter 4

Law and order

The MBO process will throw up a whole host of legal issues. Jonathan Blake, partner and head of the private equity team at S J Berwin & Co, gives an overview of some of the potential legal and practical issues that can arise in a typical buy-out transaction

The law imposes onerous responsibilities on a director with regard to his or her company, and the MBO process itself has its hurdles, for which directors should be prepared from the outset.

INITIAL STEPS

As soon as a director decides to initiate an MBO, he should approach the board. Failure to do so would give rise to conflicts of interest that could impede proper performance of his duties.

If the board is willing to contemplate an MBO, best practice suggests the following steps:

- *A board committee (excluding any director involved in the MBO and including as many non-executive directors as possible) should be formed to consider the buy-out. It may choose to instruct independent professional and financial advisers.*

- *The committee should agree with the MBO director what company information he is free to disclose to his backers.*

- *It should set guidelines for the director's future conduct and voting rights, determine how much time he can spend on the MBO and address any other potential conflicts.*

- *The board may authorise the committee to negotiate any heads of agreement with the MBO team and its backers.*

CONFLICTS OF INTEREST

Some directors or executives proposing an MBO may be reluctant to inform their employers at the outset. This will almost certainly put them at risk of breaching their employment contracts as they face many potential conflicts:

- *They have a duty not to disclose confidential information to their backers (this could damage the business and affect the price obtainable for the MBO target);*

- *They may be unable to vote at board meetings on major company issues that could adversely affect a possible MBO (their personal interests may not fully coincide with the company's);*

- *They cannot involve any colleagues in the MBO or persuade staff to join the buy-out vehicle.*

It is important to address these potential conflicts up-front. Some would be resolved if the MBO went ahead, since the seller, in selling the target to the MBO vehicle, would probably be accepting the breaches. However, if it did not proceed but the director's involvement later came to light – and meanwhile decisions had been taken or information disclosed that had damaged the company – the director could be dismissed (for blatant breaches) and/or held personally liable. Also, proposed investors in the MBO could be liable if they misused confidential company information knowing it was obtained in breach of the director's duties, or if they induced executives to breach their employment contracts.

DUTY OF THE BOARD

The board has a duty to act in the company's, shareholders' and employees' best interests and should not reject any MBO proposal outright. Where the company is a subsidiary or closely controlled, it is bound to consult its owners on any bona fide offer. If, following such consultation, the board did not agree to the proposed MBO, there would be little point in proceeding further – unless, perhaps, the transaction was a public-to-private (see Chapter 9). In other cases, the board's financial advisers might recommend putting the target up for auction to obtain the best possible terms.

CAN THE COMPANY UNDERWRITE ABORTIVE LEGAL FEES?

Target companies are prohibited from giving "financial assistance" to MBO companies acquiring their shares. It would clearly be unlawful for a company whose shares were being purchased to bear the costs of its management in a successful MBO. However, in practice, if the MBO proceeds, fees are likely to be borne by the MBO vehicle. Even where the company is asked to underwrite legal fees on an abortive attempt to purchase its own shares there may be financial assistance issues, and listed companies must not breach restrictions on giving "exceptional" indemnities without shareholder approval.

APPOINTING ADVISERS

Advisers appointed by financial backers usually lead the MBO process, and often the interests of management and backers coincide, but there will obviously be a conflict of interest on issues such as management shareholdings in the MBO vehicle and service agreements. Management will need to take advice from their own lawyers, who should have buy-out experience.

Financial backers almost always commission accountants to look at the target business. Management must devote time to co-operating, and to reading the accountants' report – they are likely to have to give warranties on its contents.

An engagement letter will be entered into with the firm preparing the report. It is now established that the "Big Six" accountancy firms will seek to cap their liability to £25m or the value of the deal, if lower. Such firms will also limit their liability proportionally on any claim. If the financial backers can only recover part of a claim from the accountants, the extent to which the MBO directors are exposed to claims by aggrieved investors must be addressed in the legal documentation.

CASE STUDY

Legal issues can bedevil any management buy-out, particularly when it comes to maintaining confidentiality and avoiding conflicts of interest.

In the JLI Group MBO, Phildrew Ventures and management were well aware of the problem and hired two law firms, one to tackle issues related to the acquisition itself and another, to look after the management contracts and deal with shareholder documentation.

Tony Orvis, Chief executive of Harrington Food Group, comments: "We felt it important to separate the two elements. We chose our lawyers, among other things, because they had previous public-to-private experience."

As a public company, Harrington and its advisers had also to consider the Takeover Panel, which imposes its own rigorous rules on all such transactions.

Yet, although the majority of MBOs are straight buy-outs, Orvis says they can prove less straightforward from a legal standpoint than public-to private-deals. "You do not have the sale and purchase agreement issues that inevitably go with such a transaction. So in my experience the legals were easier and faster," he says.

Group directors, usually anxious to ensure that the business continues to be run properly during the bid process, can insist that company directors step down before mounting a buy-out.

For JLI, this was not possible since the company was too small – and both the main executive directors, Orvis and finance director, Martyn Bishop, were involved in the buy-out. However, the nonparticipating directors formed an Independent Committee to consider bid proposals on behalf of the shareholders and ensure the business continued to be run properly.

Directors will usually lean heavily on their legal advisers, according to Orvis: "Although I had done a number of acquisitions this was my first public-to-private. This is the case for most people, as few do more than one! So I felt it was important to use advisers that were recognised for that type of work. I must say, they were absolutely first class."

LEGAL DUE DILIGENCE

The backers' lawyers will undertake a due diligence exercise, raising questions regarding the business which the management team will probably have to answer on behalf of the vendor. The vendor will also prepare a disclosure letter in collaboration with the management team.

SHAREHOLDER CONSENT

The Companies Act requires shareholders' consent to the sale of ten per cent or more of a company's net tangible assets, or assets valued at £100,000 or more, to a director of the company or its holding company or anyone connected with him (which may include the MBO vehicle). In the case of listed companies, provisions of the City Code on Takeovers and Mergers also apply, as do Stock Exchange rules on sharedealing and the law on insider dealing if directors or others are privy to unpublished price-sensitive information.

SECURITY FOR DEBT FINANCE

Private companies can, in certain circumstances, give financial assistance for acquisition of their own shares using the target company's assets as security for MBO vehicle borrowings. Most banks providing debt finance require such security.

The target company's directors will have to be able to make a statutory declaration – backed by an auditor's letter – that the company can meet debts falling due during the year following the MBO. If providing security involves any reduction in the subsidiary's net assets and therefore provision has to be made in its accounts, this would need to be covered by existing distributable profits. Public companies cannot give financial assistance but can sometimes re-register as private companies in order to enter into security arrangements.

Loans by the target company or its subsidiaries after the buy-out to help the MBO vehicle repay the buy-out loan also constitute financial assistance and require a similar procedure.

AFTER THE CHAMPAGNE

If any bank debt has been provided, there will be financial covenants in the banking documentation, within which the company will ultimately have to operate. During the MBO process the management team must study these constraints and evaluate the viability of operating within them. In due course they may also have to report to the financial investors and ensure compliance with covenants in the shareholders' agreement and banking documentation.

Chapter 5

Valuation, negotiation and structure

Ian Hawkins, Partner, Phildrew Ventures, offers tips for mastering the key ingredients of an MBO

Purchasing a company can be compared with purchasing a house. The negotiation process must ultimately present the vendor with an acceptable price, just as the purchaser must be happy that the price offered represents good value – enabling appropriate returns on investment to be made. The concept that the "right" price is that upon which the vendor and purchaser can agree is a truism, but what influences pricing and valuation decisions? Most transactions hit a number of decision points where they proceed or lapse, mostly on grounds of price.

SUBSIDENCE?

The reasons for sale can have a significant bearing on the negotiation process and the price payable. Just as a tenant may know the good and bad points of a house, so management is usually in the best position to recognise the attractions of purchasing the business they manage. However, management suffers from conflicts of interest when attempting an MBO, the resolution of which determines the nature of subsequent negotiations.

Loyalties become divided: on the one hand the buy-out teams should pursue self-interest and negotiate for the lowest possible purchase price by exploiting their knowledge; on the other, they should remember that they are negotiating with shareholders, ultimately their employers, whose interests they are expected to represent and with whom relationships may have to be maintained

- either because the sale falls through or because of trading relationships which subsequently survive the transaction.

In these circumstances the importance of working with experienced venture capital funding sources and advisers cannot be over emphasised, and the earlier they are involved the better. Their involvement can protect management from the worst of the conflicts and can encourage the vendor to appreciate the advantages of giving management first option rather than pursuing an expensive auction process. Fees can be saved, the sale can be discrete and avoid exposure of business details to competitors and – because of inside knowledge – deals can be completed quickly at good prices.

FOOT IN THE DOOR

The MBO process has changed considerably. Whereas once a deserving management team could negotiate favourable purchase terms with their parent company, today levels of competition are such that the prime negotiation is between vendor and the private equity house which arranges and funds the transaction.

Nevertheless, at the first inkling that a parent is likely to consider selling a company, management should put down a marker. An initial approach to funding sources is best made with parental approval and will hopefully pre-empt the commencement of a widely-marketed auction process. The key to success at this point is flexibility to structure the deal in order to address the vendor's sensitivities and requirements quickly and discreetly.

As information starts to flow and statistics pile up, all sides will be seeking to identify pricing parameters. Views will be formed on what should be an acceptable price based upon the vendor's position, his need for cash, the impact on his earnings and the value of the target company to any other potential competing bidders.

At the same time, the venture capitalist will form initial views of what is affordable, based upon the financial information available, both historic and projected, the attractions of the target company, its products, markets and management. These all combine to paint a picture from which he can anticipate his funding structure and the returns available subject to achieving projected performance. He will also rapidly form a view of what return is required for the level of risk being assumed.

PRICING MODEL

Simplistically, the funding structure and pricing is driven by determining the maximum level of funding available from each source:

■ *Bank debt is generally determined by the ability to repay, focusing on cashflow and the ability to pay interest and make repayments within a sensible timescale. However, in a capital intensive company asset backing may also be important. Recent developments in capital markets have generated new products such as high yield bonds which provide greater flexibility in terms of gearing levels and repayment terms particularly for larger transactions.*

■ *Equity is predominately sourced from the venture capitalist who will build his return around a mix of income, capital repayment – if cashflows allow – and capital gain. The mix of ordinary shares and other instruments gear up management's equity interest disproportionately to their cash contribution, but that percentage is predominately driven by the return requirements of the venture capitalist.*

The impact of financial gearing on the participants in a simplified transactions might be as follows:

Take a company which is making operating profits of £15m, growing at around 10 per cent per annum, which might be valued in today's markets at £150m debt free. In order to achieve this growth the company will have to invest, adding fixed assets (ie. in excess of, say, £5m per annum of depreciation) and working capital (net of efficiency savings) of, say, £2m per annum. In this scenario a debt package of £80m might be secured with repayments being made over eight to ten years and interest charged at a 2 per cent margin over LIBOR, ie. around 7 per cent per annum. Overall cashflows could therefore follow the pattern outlined in the box:

£000's	Historical	Year 1	Year 2	Year 3	Year 4
Operating profit	15	17	19	21	23
Depreciation	5	5	6	6	6
Investment	(7)	(7)	(8)	(8)	(8)
Operating cashflow	13	15	17	19	21
Interest		(6)	(5)	(4)	(4)
Tax	-		(3)	(4)	(5)
Net debt reduction		9	9	11	12

After four years the £80m of initial bank debt will therefore have halved to below £40m.

If we now assume that the company is sold on similar multiples for £230m there is maybe £188m to share amongst the equity participants after expenses. The venture capitalist will have provided some £72m, the vast bulk of which will be in a loan note or preference share earning a fixed compound return.

The balance will be split between ordinary shareholders – management, venture capitalist and, if included, any providers of mezzanine debt. In this example the split might be 15:85 to give management a healthy £13.2m for such a successful exit.

To summarise, the amounts provided at the outset and received on exit would be:

£m			Subscribed	At exit
Ordinary Shares – Management	(15%)		0.3	13.2
– VC	(85%)		1.7	74.8
10% Loan Notes – VC			70.0	100.0
Bank Debt			80.0	39.0
Expenses			–	3.0
			152.0	230.0

Thus management turns £300,000 into £13.2m and the venture capitalist £71.7m into £174.8m – a return of around 25 per cent per annum. However, the assumptions made might not allow so much debt or such high returns and the structuring process must be rejuggled by an interactive process until the mix of the purchase price, debt levels, realisation assumptions and returns all balance.

CASE STUDY

Dr Julian Blogh knew better than to underpay when it came to discussing the price tag for the seven electronics businesses he wanted to buy from TI.

The group made it clear that it had other potential buyers lined up for all seven of the businesses, and even getting exclusive negotiating rights had been a challenge. In the end Phildrew, Montagu and Arthur Andersen came up with the price tag between them. "Forty million pounds sounded like an awful lot of money to me, but it was the figure our advisers arrived at," says Blogh.

This figure was offered to TI on almost the first day of negotiations, subject to an adjustment for the value of net assets to be transferred. The company eventually transferred £24.25m of net assets. Further agreement was required on transferring potentially ruinous liabilities from overseas defence contracts to TI. "Funnily enough, the headline price itself was not really an issue," says Blogh. "We haggled over the net assets rather than the price."

Dowty's and then TI's ownership of Dowty Electronics had been typical of many reluctant parents – it had never been treated as a core operation and had only had second call on investment resources.

Blogh's initial caution regarding the businesses' potential later proved unwarranted: "I never realised quite how cash-generative the businesses were until we came to run them after the MBO. Good cash generation has proved to be our strength. There was much more pent-up cash in the business than we realised, and that gave us the potential to grow."

Blogh's investment – "meaningful rather than significant" – was less than he had anticipated but reflected his circumstances. He had taken a big risk by resigning to make the bid happen, although he admits that restructuring would have caused him to become redundant in due course anyway. "Had the bid failed I'd personally have had a problem as a fifty-something former company director," he says.

NEGOTIATING WITH THE VENDOR

Having confirmed some interest in a sale and persuaded a venture capitalist to join forces, negotiations can commence.

Price will be the major consideration and it would be usual to indicate a range which has, at its top end, the figure emerging from the pricing model. This assumes all good news and few contingencies. If management gets a shot at an exclusive bid, it needs to put its best foot forward to avoid the vendor seeking other bids to ensure it does its duty to secure the best price.

If the indicative price is in the right "ball-park" the haggling ensues. Price tends to make way for comfort factors and the MBO can gain advantage by being willing to take problems – which they can understand and quantify – off the vendor's hands. These problems – which may include a loss making subsidiary, or an exposure to some historic event – could put off competing bidders.

In many instances the vendor will have a need to secure a headline price which cannot readily be justified. In this case the vendor will often be offered some deferred consideration or a residual stake.

In the example above, the vendor might retain a 25 per cent stake receiving a net figure of £128.9m (ie, £150m less 25/85ths of £71.7m) for apparently selling 75 per cent of the company implying a valuation of almost £172m versus the £150m above. Alternatively, the deferred consideration may only be payable when a future event or performance benchmark has occurred which helps justify the higher price.

DUE DILIGENCE

Eventually the MBO team should seek to secure agreement in principle and an exclusivity period during which it will investigate the company and complete the transaction without fear of being "gazumped" by another offer. The results of due diligence may allow the offer to be confirmed, but possibly with conditions attached – and this may generate further negotiation. If significant problems are identified the offer price may be revised – the parallel being with a house survey.

COMPLETION

The process culminates, after several weeks, in a completion meeting at which all elements of the transaction are pulled together. Despite significant preparation, negotiations often continue until all documents are signed and all disclosures made, most compromises being made after midnight!

In the aftermath of completion, the champagne flows and all thoughts of pricing and negotiation fade. Management have secured their own independent castle until their "exit" looms when management and venture capitalist themselves become vendors seeking maximum valuation via a trade sale or alternatively by stepping up to become a quoted company.

Chapter 6

The crucial role of independent advisers

Martin Kitcatt, head of private equity at Arthur Andersen's Corporate Finance group, points out the "must-have" attributes of independent advisers and outlines their role in the buy-out process

Going through a buy-out is enough to severely test the nerves of the toughest management team. While today's buy-out environment is highly favourable for the aggressive and ambitious, it is also very competitive. Venture capitalists are becoming ever more focused on the size and sector in which they invest, new funding ideas are emerging, investment criteria are changing rapidly, and many deals cross international boundaries.

TIME, TIME AND MORE TIME

A consistent fact about buy-outs is that they are extremely time-consuming and generate a lot of stress. An independent adviser's key role is to allow you to remain focused on your business by project-managing each step of the process, from conceptualisation to completion and beyond. They will control the compilation of business plans, deal structures and fundraising, negotiate with the vendor, and advise on selecting and concluding the optimal deal. As well as devising timetables and liaising with lawyers and others, they will prioritise tasks so that you can maintain control of the transaction spending minimum time away from ongoing business.

With the multitude of advisers in the marketplace, how do you select the best one to work with? And what exactly should you be asking of them? The first thing to look for is experience.

Your potential independent adviser should understand current market conditions, be respected within the financial community and have a solid track record.

However, all this is useless without "chemistry". You will be spending months with these people and you need to trust and respect them. Their advice will often extend beyond mere professional opinion. In terms of responsibility, the independent adviser's job consists of two key stages:

- *Preparation: This includes conducting a detailed feasibility assessment and helping to draft the business plan or information memorandum.*

- *Execution: Devising the deal structure, raising finances, negotiating with the vendor and other parties, planning future growth post-deal and forecasting exit options.*

PREPARATION

The preparation phase – the most crucial aspect of any management buy-out– begins with the feasibility assessment, in which your advisers give an honest opinion on the validity of your proposal. The experienced adviser will quickly grasp the finer details of your business, spot potential funding issues, offer constructive criticism and counsel you on the personal and professional risks (and rewards) that lie ahead.

The feasibility assessment is vital to all parties because it establishes whether the buy-out can work at the right price for both purchaser and vendor in the current marketplace. This involves preparing an initial valuation based on projections. The best advisers will not let the deal move ahead at an inflated price, and will explain in detail how they've reached the valuation level.

Next, the advisers help you create your passport to raising money – the business plan. Using existing five-year plans and budget forecasts, they must put together a document conveying all the necessary business information in a "financier-friendly" format to attract optimum investor interest.

A typical business plan covers the following:

■ *Executive summary – A concise round-up to whet the funder's appetite;*

■ *Background and history – Explaining why the opportunity has arisen;*

■ *Products or services – What you do and how you sell;*

■ *Production and supply – How you make or deliver what you do;*

■ *Markets and competition – An overview of your current marketplace, where you fit into it, developments and trends;*

■ *Management team – Who you are and why you should be backed;*

■ *Personnel – Key personnel and human resources strategy;*

■ *Risks and opportunities – An honest appraisal...nothing is risk-free;*

■ *Financial details – The cornerstone of your proposal...no latitude for error;*

■ *Deal structure – Plans for the funding structure.*

Be prepared to spend time on your business plan. It is the benchmark on which the deal is structured and against which the company will be measured post-deal.

EXECUTION

Armed with an airtight business plan, devoid of ambiguity and loaded with detail, the next step is to execute the buy-out. Of utmost importance is structuring a deal with which you are completely comfortable and which meets your strategic and long-term objectives. Deal structuring is often an exercise in compromise and advisers must be adept at accommodating the views of financiers and management within operating, tax and legal constraints. Communication is important – your advisers

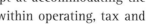

should be proactive in explaining the options available and why certain funding avenues are non-viable. This is also the time to consider the best exit options for any deal structure.

You can now enter the marketplace in search of financing. Today's buy-out environment features a host of interested parties almost unknown five years ago, so up-to-date market knowledge is crucial. The careful selection of potential funders is based on a combination of experience, sector specialisation, size and, again, chemistry. You should aim for the same open relationship as you have with your advisers.

At this stage your advisers' role is to pinpoint financial backers with a genuine interest in your business and its plans. They will have both qualitative and quantitative understanding of what constitutes the best investment package for all parties and should explain how much you will be investing, for what equity stake and under what conditions, as well as what relationship to expect after completion of the deal.

Developments now move swiftly. It's highly likely that negotiations with various parties will commence while talks progress with financial backers. This is to the buy-out team's benefit: if a backer suddenly pulls out, your advisers can quickly bring in alternative financing. Advisers can play a pivotal role by acting as lead negotiator with the vendor – a common occurrence today as vendors and management teams seek to protect their relationships in case no deal is agreed.

With confidentiality a given, advisers will suggest various negotiating strategies and tactics to leverage your strengths and minimise identified weaknesses. And although price is important, there are other factors to consider, such as supply and service agreements and pension and healthcare plans. There's also the challenge of handling multiple negotiations simultaneously to tight deadlines – with the vendor and its advisers, lawyers and actuaries, with venture capitalists, banks and their teams. Your advisers should keep you constantly abreast of developments, with the aim of keeping negotiations smooth and effective.

THE END IS ONLY THE BEGINNING

You thought that was hard work? Your next task is to deliver on your advisers' and backers' belief that you can grow the company's value. The business plan that acted as your passport to financial support now becomes your game-plan for success. Short-term plans should already be under way, with your longer-term exit option always in view. Remember – not only will your financial backers use the business plan as a benchmark, but ultimately it reflects the value of the independent advisers that helped you put it together.

CASE STUDY

When Julian Blogh, newly resigned from Dowty, went for preliminary talks with TI, the company tried imposing some fearsome conditions on him.

Even his choice of legal advisers was restricted to firms that TI had never worked with. "As you can imagine that limited the choice somewhat," observes Blogh wryly. "In the end they accepted that their shortlist was too short and relented. We were allowed to appoint Clifford Chance."

Blogh's key advisers throughout the process, however, were Arthur Andersen. "I appointed them because they had audited parts of Dowty and knew the businesses, knew the industry."

Blogh's resignation from Dowty meant he was able to focus full-time on the bid and did not have the distraction of running the business at the same time. Even so, there were several near-breakdowns in the process. "It wouldn't have succeeded had my financial advisers not been there. Whenever negotiations came to an impasse, which they did frequently, Andersen were there to pick it all up again."

Blogh recalls that the beauty parades to select advisers were extensive for some parts of the deal, while in others – such as tax – experts came highly recommended. He used Andersen's in-house tax specialists. "We went to see several venture capitalists, for instance, but some rejected us and we didn't like the look of others.

He believes the quality of the relationship with his key advisers was crucial. "It sounds strange, but you have to get on. It's very important. After you've been through the hard negotiations with your venture capitalists, you then find yourselves both on the same side of the table negotiating hard with the bankers on the other side. If you're not sure who your friends are, it can make for a pretty intense situation."

Chapter 7

Banking on the transaction

Craig Wilson, head of structured finance with the Bank of Scotland, explains the strategy for successful MBO partnerships from the banking viewpoint

Not every manager or director gets the opportunity to participate in a MBO, but those who do, should experience a unique dynamic environment in which to take their businesses forward as owner-entrepreneurs with a view to creating value. The MBO process is a profoundly meaningful experience for any management team – and one that is materially enhanced by ensuring that the right partners are chosen from the outset.

Other key parties to the MBO, such as advisers and private equity sponsors, are discussed in other chapters. This one addresses selection of the right banking partner.

THE BANK AS PARTNER IN THE TRANSACTION

While most companies will be comfortable with their existing banking relationships, it should be accepted early in the MBO process that existing bankers may not be fully equipped to provide the level of service required both during and after the transaction.

Banks experienced in management buy-outs will have the appropriate resources, creativity and knowledge to add value to the transaction process and to provide ongoing support to the company's management in the post-MBO environment. Through its advisers and equity partners, the MBO team will be introduced to banks that have proven experience and valid credentials in the MBO market.

A bank that has demonstrated a commitment to this market over time is well placed to help an MBO team through the transaction process. It can meet the team's needs not only during the buy-out itself but also in the post-MBO phase, when an understanding relationship will be required to ease the company through its period of change. In general, and certainly where indigenous banks are involved, the bank that completes the MBO is more often than not the one that will take this relationship forward, utilising its network of corporate offices to satisfy the company's local banking needs and preferences.

HOW BANKS CAN ADD VALUE

An experienced bank will demonstrate certain key characteristics which, properly applied, should sustain its activities in the MBO market by defining its presence and its ability to add value. These characteristics can be summarised as the five Cs:

- *Consistency;*

- *Coherency;*

- *Certainty;*

- *Creativity;*

- *Constancy.*

CONSISTENCY

To be effective over the longer term, banks must be able to sustain a position whereby they consistently effect buy-ins and buy-outs rather than dipping in and out of the market. In developing quality relationships with corporate customers, advisers and equity sponsors, there is little value in banks being in the market one year and out of it the next.

Conscious of market trends and economic cycles, an effective bank will work around these by adopting long-term lending policies and tailoring lending parameters to different types of business. It will structure transactions on the basis of detailed knowledge of the profile of each business and of the impact of cycles and seasonality.

If a bank can demonstrate consistency in its lending standards, it is likely to make good lending decisions. It is in its interest to do so, as each successful outcome helps the bank maintain its market presence, and banks with a successful track record are looked on more positively within the market.

COHERENCY

An effective bank will be able to convey a coherent message regarding its lending policies and outlook on business partnerships – and be able to back this up at all times. No question should ever arise as to a bank's appetite for business because of a lack of consistency or coherency.

CERTAINTY

A bank is well placed in the MBO market when its partners on the advisory or equity side can say: "We know our partners at the bank will like this transaction and be able to deliver, providing us with certainty of funds." Anything less and the parties choosing a bank are taking undue risk in attempting to ensure that funds will be available at completion.

Deliverability is a key feature in how banks are perceived. It is quite common, when banks are tendering to become involved in a management buy-out, for the bank offering the most debt and the best terms not to be selected, particularly if it is considered the least likely to deliver at completion.

CREATIVITY

Management buy-outs are rarely straightforward and the structure of the financing is prone to change many times during the transaction process.

Banks not only have to be aware of this but must be prepared to react quickly, effectively and with flexibility. Rapid decision-making and short lines of communication are key factors to the buy-out's success. By the very nature of their operating culture, banks that are flexible are those whose staff are most likely to be capable of creativity.

CASE STUDY

Ultra Electronics has been a runaway success since the MBO. But such a conclusion was far from obvious to the bankers who lined up to underwrite the company's debt at the outset.

Julian Blogh admits that if he were to restart the whole process with the benefit of hindsight, he'd pay greater attention to the process of choosing bankers. "We had a bank consortium arranging the senior debt, five or six in fact. Each time one had to go to a higher level in their organisation for approval there would be a problem. Invariably it happened on Bank Holiday weekends, and we'd be left with an extra day in which to worry."

Ultra's lead banker was the Bank of Scotland. Although it was committed to the transaction, it had, on two separate occasions, three months apart, to find new bankers to take part in the consortium after others pulled out.

"Appointing bankers was a fraught process. When we spoke to individuals they always appeared enthusiastic. Several went halfway but then we were referred to higher powers in the banks, only to be turned down flat," he says. "Some banks were already exposed to the aerospace and defence sectors and didn't want any more risk."

The financing was complicated by the fact that Montagu Private Equity, which with Phildrew Ventures backed Blogh's team, was being absorbed by HSBC at the time. "It became clear to me that venture capitalists were not the problem once we were well down the line. It's the solid commitment of bankers that you need.

"When you're new to the process you don't know how much room you have to negotiate with bankers. I would spend more time on the selection process if I did it again," he admits. "The system worked well for us eventually and it probably sounds churlish to criticise now. But I think it's a reflection of how we felt at the time when they were pulling out on us."

CONSTANCY

This is the bottom line for the bank, encompassing all the other Cs in creating an environment centred on trust, high professional standards and effective partnership. Whilst equity sponsors and advisers will recognise the features of a quality bank and introduce it to buy-outs on that basis, ultimately the bank's virtues should shine through into the relationship with the MBO team and the new company long after the transaction is completed.

THE BANK/MANAGEMENT RELATIONSHIP

For a bank to demonstrate fully the characteristics that are critical to the transaction process and to operate effectively in the MBO market, it has to be able to quickly develop a solid relationship with the team in order to satisfy itself as to their capabilities, integrity and commitment. But this is clearly a two-way street – at the same time the bank must demonstrate the same characteristics to management.

Throughout the MBO process the bank will make every effort to ensure that it understands the business. It can and will obtain as much information as it needs to make the ultimate judgement on whether the risks are acceptable in relation to the funds being advanced. This can only be achieved in an environment where information flows freely and honestly against a background of intent to achieve full disclosure.

Carefully prepared plans and proposals are essential to the process, as is management's detailed knowledge of all the elements backing up such information. Last-minute surprises are dangerous and unwelcome in the MBO process. Early disclosure of relevant issues is essential, as a creative and flexible bank will work to address these and incorporate their impact into the transaction structure.

Management and the bank will be developing their relationship throughout the transaction process and it is important that this is built upon towards completion of the MBO. To throw in another couple of Cs – Complete Candour is essential in forming a sound basis for trust and understanding, which will help all concerned in the years ahead.

GOING FORWARD

When choosing banking partners, MBO teams should bear in mind that a quality bank endeavours to foster mutually fruitful long-term relationships with all of its customers. The bank's recognition and understanding of the company's business and strategic issues will help to engender an effective co-operative approach in good times as well as during difficult periods. Together, the MBO team and the bank can work as a creative combination towards the successful achievement of everyone's goals.

Chapter 8

What is due diligence?

Richard Green, transaction services partner at PricewaterhouseCoopers, outlines the due diligence exercise and clarifies its role in the ultimate success of the deal

Private equity investors are facing greater challenges than ever before in their search for the best deals in the buy-out arena. This inevitably places greater pressure on the management teams participating in buy-outs, for most of whom this is a once-in-a-lifetime experience – one that, while ultimately rewarding, can initially be frustrating and even exhausting.

The challenges in today's deal environment are characterised by strictly controlled auction processes, increasing competition, rising deal values, higher gearing, complex deal structures and an increase in public-to-private transactions. All these factors combine to heighten the risk profile attached to today's buy-out. The margin for error within deals is now very small, and consequently the need for comprehensive and effective due diligence is heightened.

MITIGATING RISKS

So what is due diligence, and how can it relieve pressure, reduce frustration and mitigate the risks faced by the management team? A due diligence assignment should be more than a simplistic analysis of the target's historical financial results. It should be a robust independent enquiry capable of enhancing both the MBO team and the financial backers' understanding of the company and its key business drivers, identifying areas of negotiating strength and weakness, quantifying and minimising risks, and above all highlighting areas where value can be delivered.

An effective due diligence will achieve the following five goals:

- *Confirm the absence of "black holes";*

- *Expose the underlying reality of the historical track record;*

- *Give clear opinions on the target company's current status and prospects;*

- *Highlight negotiating issues and potential deal-breakers;*

- *Lead to an action plan for transition of the business so as to maximise value.*

In today's environment access is often restricted in the early stages. Consequently, initial due diligence will depend on an analysis of information provided, together with other publicly available information, to highlight key issues impacting on the deal and matters to be addressed during exclusivity.

Auction processes are often supported by the preparation of a sell-side due diligence report, commissioned by the vendor at the beginning of the sale process for provision to prospective purchasers. The objective is to provide all bidders with similar information derived from a single due diligence process. This limits management disruption at the target company while giving the vendor greater control over the information flow. Regardless of the type of due diligence, it should still address the five main goals listed above.

BLACK HOLES

Agreement in principle to proceed with a transaction is normally made following discussions between the vendor, its advisers, private equity investors, financing institutions, and last but not least the management team. An independent review will not normally have been conducted at this stage. Decisions will typically be based on a preliminary evaluation of the target's business, based on information supplied and representations given by the management team.

In response to the realities of the timetable, a phased approach to the due diligence is often effective in identifying any black holes early on, before the management team and financial backers commit additional time and resource. The first phase will usually involve an initial assessment providing rapid feedback and involving fact-finding and an assessment of key assumptions, value, price and any potential deal-breaking issues.

HISTORICAL TRACK RECORD

The focus on historical results in acquiring a company could cynically be compared to using only a rear-view mirror when driving a car. Clearly what is being acquired in the transaction is the target's ability to generate profits in the future and to grow the business from its existing position. However, since many of the key assumptions underlying the valuation of a deal are underpinned by the target's historical results, a thorough understanding of the business drivers influencing them is necessary to evaluate the basis for the deal. Furthermore, management's past achievements can be a persuasive indication of potential future performance.

The work to uncover the underlying reality of historical data is normally carried out in phase two of the due diligence, when access to management is critical. It involves detailed consultation with the target company, including the financial, operational and commercial management teams. The objective is to obtain an in-depth understanding of trends affecting the target's revenue streams and costs.

The analysis of financial information as part of the due diligence should not be confused with an audit. It should result in an incisive commentary containing commercial judgements on the fundamentals of the business, highlighting negotiating issues and potential deal-breakers.

CURRENT STATUS AND PROSPECTS

Due diligence should focus on the target's current status and prospects to make sure that investors know what they are buying and that their rationale for supporting the company's future growth and development is sound. The acquisition decision is based primarily on anticipated future performance, so a clear picture of management's plans for the business will allow the assumptions underlying their projections to be vigorously challenged. This will require discussion with the whole management team, following which all areas of concern or doubt, plus upside potential, will be brought to the attention of the team and its financiers. This will normally be supported by a sensitivity analysis outlining the impact on projected profits and cashflows of changes in the assumptions. This is often critical in a buy-out where the cashflows must be capable of supporting the financing and absorbing potential trading vulnerabilities.

NEGOTIATING ISSUES AND POTENTIAL DEAL-BREAKERS

The due diligence will typically be led by transaction services specialists drawing on in-house expertise to review all the assumptions underlying the deal – including specialists in strategy, tax, pensions, HR and operational areas.

The involvement of these various specialists should ensure that a product of the due diligence is a summary of all the deal issues, encompassing negotiating issues and potential deal-breakers, that need to be considered in completing the transaction.

TRANSITION OF THE BUSINESS

The due diligence exercise provides an opportunity (not to be wasted) to draw on the expertise of commercially-minded accountants who can provide a robust independent commentary on the fundamentals of the business. It can add value to the deal by leading to an action plan for transition of the acquired business.

SUMMARY

Respecting time constraints, the due diligence findings should be communicated clearly and concisely in the form of robust commercial opinions on the risks and uncertainties of the business and the key value drivers of the deal.

The due diligence exercise places an additional burden on all members of the management team, not just the financial management, and is often viewed as a necessary evil. For confidentiality reasons, it is often difficult for senior management to delegate their involvement in the process to other members of the management team. However, since the completion of due diligence is normally a precondition of financial backers' support for the buy-out, it is essential to devote sufficient time and attention to it.

Due diligence should help to maximise the return on the deal by ensuring that equity investors, debt providers and management are clear about exactly what they are buying, and that the potential downside – as well as the upside – is fully reflected in the value of the deal.

CASE STUDY

Due diligence is the investors' safety net, the process by which they are protected from potential pitfalls. Close examination of the target company focuses not just on its financial health but on all the potential liabilities facing the business.

Although the extent and length of due diligence varies from deal to deal, it typically takes four to six weeks for a straightforward MBO at a subsidiary of a quoted plc, but can take longer if the business itself is a public-to-private transaction and conducts business from many different semi-autonomous locations, each of which will require close study.

In any case, due diligence begins on an informal basis as soon as accountants are appointed. Issues such as pensions or environmental issues are not usually potential dealbreakers. They're pricing issues. Of more concern to the would-be backer is current trading. On a purely financial basis, due diligence examines the industry in which the company competes, the profitability of the business, its recent track record, the accounting policies in use and – particularly – its treatment of cash.

This latter point is important since the price paid for the company will hinge on the proportion of debt and cash held in the business at the time of the transaction. Underperformance during the bid process is unnerving for backers as it can raise questions about directors' abilities. Their credibility can be blown if they can't even adhere to next month's targets.

For Harrington Food Group's backers, due diligence was particularly important, since mounting losses and difficulties at the group's snacks business Tee Gee over the previous three years meant there could have been black holes elsewhere that the subsidiary's problems were helping to conceal.

By the time the deal is ready to be signed, there should be no part of the business that has not been opened up to scrutiny.

Chapter 9

Buy-outs of public companies

In recent years the number of public-to-private transactions has increased. **Bernard Jolles, director of Campbell Lutyens & Co Ltd, goes into the intricacies of this relatively new type of deal**

Public-to-private takeovers (PTPs) generally take the form of private equity-financed MBOs. Sometimes listed companies are taken private by families with large controlling shareholdings, and in such cases the role of management is also pivotal. PTPs are usually initiated by either the management team or a private equity group, but occasionally they are a response to a third-party bid approach or suggested by a major shareholder.

PTPs combine the features of a normal MBO and a public takeover where the rules of the Takeover Code apply. The Code is designed to protect shareholders' interests and ensure that all shareholders are treated equally. The PTP deal process and associated risks therefore differ from a normal MBO in certain ways and are more complex.

THE PUBLIC-TO-PRIVATE DEAL PROCESS

Control of the public company changes after shareholders' acceptance of a formal offer (or a scheme of arrangement) for their shares. Before announcing this and posting the offer document, the bidder needs to complete the following steps:

- *Agree the offer price with independent directors and their advisers;*

- *Obtain support for the offer from major shareholders;*

- *Complete a due diligence review;*

- *Establish the PTP vehicle and arranged unconditionally committed equity and debt finance.*

INDEPENDENT DIRECTORS

An early step is for the target's board to appoint a committee of independent directors (with no ongoing role within the PTP vehicle) to consider the PTP and any competing proposals. These directors will appoint financial advisers (so-called Rule 3 advisers) to advise them on the proposals and support any recommendations or views expressed to shareholders – in whose best interests they are obliged to act. Early decisions will be whether the MBO directors should be permitted to explore the PTP and the ground rules for their doing so.

The Code requires finance for the offer to be unconditionally committed before the offer is announced. The supply of information to the MBO's funders is therefore critical. However, any of the target's information supplied to one bidder (the MBO team and its funders) must also be supplied to competing bona fide bidders.

Given the commercial sensitivity of certain information, the independent directors must consider how much information to give the management team and its funders and when to make it available. Information (such as the MBO business plan) supplied by the MBO directors to their funders must be available to the independent directors. However, this information will not be seen by competing bidders.

SECRECY

The Code requires absolute secrecy before an offer is announced and also places restrictions on the number of potential funders that can be approached.

If there is an "untoward" share price movement (10 per cent above the lowest price after the initial approach), the Panel is likely to require announcement of a bid approach. This effectively puts the company into play and is unhelpful to the buy-out attempt.

OFFER PRICE

The offer price is agreed in principle at an early stage between the MBO and the independent directors (and possibly major shareholders). It will be conditional on satisfactory due diligence and completion of the financing arrangements. Questions that may affect the price include the following:

- *What is the share price history and have any shareholders indicated an acceptable price level?*

- *How will market price movements influence the negotiating process?*

- *How large is the offer price premium (if any) to the pre-bid market price?*

- *If a counter bidder emerges, is there scope to increase the offer price and still meet the funders' return criteria?*

SHAREHOLDER SUPPORT

With a normal MBO negotiations are effectively bilateral. With a PTP, the vendors are all the target's shareholders, to whom the public offer must be made. Price negotiations are undertaken with the independent directors, who may be prepared to recommend the PTP offer, but the final outcome lies with the shareholders.

The bidder must obtain at least half the target's shares before the offer can become unconditional. Depending on banking arrangements, at least 75 per cent acceptance is usually required and often 90 per cent (at which level dissident shareholders can be forced to sell).

It is therefore fundamental for the MBO directors and their funders to establish the level of shareholder support early on and convert this into offer acceptances (or share sales) when the offer emerges. In making the assessment at various stages, the following factors are relevant:

- *What level of acceptances does the bidder and its financiers require – 50 per cent, 75 per cent, 90 per cent?*

■ *What is the composition of the register of shareholders?*

■ *Will the main shareholders agree in principle to accept the offer?*

■ *Will they give undertakings to accept it? Hard (binding even if a higher bid is made) or soft undertakings?*

■ *Will it be possible to buy shares in the market? At what stage?*

■ *Will any shareholders block the deal or sell to a counterbidder?*

COUNTERBID RISK

The risk of a third party offering a higher price is perhaps the greatest uncertainty. PTPs do not usually result from a formal auction process, but the target directors have a duty to obtain the best deal for shareholders. The MBO team therefore faces the risk of a higher bid emerging during negotiations, or even after the offer document has been posted.

In assessing the risk of a counterbid, several factors must be considered:

■ *Will the offer price be perceived to be "low"?*

■ *Are there any identifiable trade buyers in the UK or overseas?*

■ *Is a third-party counterbid against the incumbent management likely?*

■ *Has the company recently been a takeover target?*

■ *Will the target provide exclusivity by agreeing not to solicit other bids?*

COSTS

Total costs on completion of a PTP (including those incurred by the target) can amount to 7–10 per cent of total financing for smaller deals and are effectively borne by the PTP vehicle. If the deal aborts, the level of costs depends on when, and the extent

CASE STUDY

Public-to-private transactions have seen a resurgence as share ratings of small companies have dropped over the past 18 months.

Small food producers such as JLI have been particularly hard hit. JLI's problems stemmed from difficulties in its snack foods business, Tee Gee. This was closed in December 1996, but the costs of doing this led to heavy losses.

The company's management buy-out was prompted by a major investor who told JLI's chief executive Tony Orvis that it wanted to get out.

"I wasn't appointed to do a buy-out, but people told me they thought it was time for a change," he says. "We couldn't go to the market for funds, debt wasn't an option and at least by being out of the City limelight we could push ahead without constantly worrying about the share price.

"The pressure to deliver better results every six months is akin to running 100-metre races. Some day you're going to be under the weather and run slower than you did before, but the City expects improvement every time. It just wasn't realistic."

Most shareholders therefore received Orvis's MBO offer with enthusiasm. The £25.3m cash bid, worth 65p a share, represented a premium of 60.5 per cent over the JLI price before the market got wind of a deal.

Phildrew Ventures and co-investors took 74.7 per cent of the ordinary shares in return for a £17.7m input, including £17.2m for preference shares and loan notes.

Orvis and two colleagues, Barry Colgate and Martyn Bishop, formed Harrington Food Group and put in £150,000 for a 24 per cent stake. Campbell Lutyens, financial adviser to Harrington, took a 1.3 per cent stake and the Bank of Scotland put up £30m of debt.

"Some investors might not have been happy with the price, given where they came in," concedes Orvis. "But realistically it was their only prospect of realising some gains in the short-to-medium term."

to which fees are contingent or phased. Abort costs are usually borne by the equity provider, with the MBO directors not required to contribute unless they have significant shareholdings.

A purchase of target shares (or an option) would give the PTP vehicle some protection against abort costs if a third party was prepared to pay a higher price. Any purchase would have to comply with the Code and insider dealing legislation.

Alternatively it could agree a profit-sharing arrangement with a major shareholder whereby it would be paid a proportion of the shareholder's additional profit in the event of a successful higher counterbid. Large management shareholders will sometimes provide this form of cost protection. Other possibilities include limited inducement or break fees paid by the target in the event of a higher third-party bid and insurance against abort costs (limited cover against a deal aborting for reasons beyond the PTP vehicle's control).

MANAGEMENT TEAM INCENTIVES

Most MBOs incentivise the management team through compensation arrangements including some form of equity participation. Similar arrangements are used in PTPs, which must be fully disclosed in the offer document. The Panel will want to ensure that the management team directors are not getting a "special deal" and this normally involves the Rule 3 advisers confirming that the arrangements are fair and reasonable.

Chapter 10

Institutional buy-outs

Quintin Barry (partner) and Dan Jones (assistant director) of the Private Equity Advisory Group at Deloitte & Touche Corporate Finance explain how IBOs have opened up opportunities for management to participate in deals from which they might otherwise have been excluded

The institutional buy-out (IBO) is now a common type of deal in the venture capital market. An IBO is a deal where the financial institution acts as principal in negotiating and completing the deal, rather than simply being "the money" facilitating it. This contrasts with the traditional MBO or MBI, where the management team and their advisers help the institution formulate the business plan, finance structure and negotiating strategy.

WHY THE INCREASE IN IBOS?
There are two main reasons why IBOs have become more popular. One is a buy-side factor: the increased level of venture capital funding available and consequent impact on the investment approach. The other is a sell-side factor: vendor discomfort with management buy-outs, particularly on larger transactions.

As so often in the venture capital market, the trend towards IBOs began in the US before emerging here. In the US the term "leveraged buy-out" (LBO) has always been used rather than the more manager-friendly acronym MBO, reflecting a greater focus on US institutions as owners. The rise of IBOs as European venture capital funds grow towards US levels – with billion-dollar funds targeting the European market – means that few deals are now beyond the reach of venture capitalists.

HIGHER FUNDING, BIGGER DEALS

The announcement of large new funds and very public (in every sense) deals with venture capitalists fighting each other for control of large businesses – eg. the battle for Hillsdown between Hicks Muse and Candover – have caught the attention of major corporates and their advisers. The success of some recent auctions has been such that major investment banks running auctions now actively court venture capitalists, which in the past they often seemed to regard as buyers of the last resort.

There are a number of practical reasons why institutions are taking the driving seat on certain, typically large, transactions. On larger deals the cash a management team can contribute towards financing a transaction is insignificant in terms of overall deal size. Nevertheless, if management's input to the bid process can be accessed it will be valued.

Funds focusing on larger deals tend to make relatively few investments and expect every one to succeed, in contrast to those who do a higher volume of smaller-sized deals and adopt a portfolio approach to investment. Executives in such funds therefore take the initiative rather than settling for a passive role. The "carry" they have in these deals brings the potential for substantial personal rewards and is all the more significant on large transactions.

There is an argument that institutions can afford to be less concerned about management in larger deals. First, because a large-scale business has critical mass, strong systems and management strength in depth, reducing the importance of individuals.

Second, the scale of the business also makes it easier to recruit strong new management from outside. However, this does not make incumbent management unimportant – due diligence will focus heavily on their capabilities. It is simply that on large transactions the difference between excellent and average management means the difference between excellent and average returns, while on smaller, less robust ones it can mean the difference between success and business failure. Finally, the venture capitalist may also seek to complement the existing management team with a "big hitter" to create a Buy-in management buy-out (BIMBO).

VENDOR ATTITUDES

Certain aspects of MBOs have always made vendors uncomfortable – particularly perceived conflicts of interest among management teams. This partly explains why competitive auctions have become more commonplace. In these auctions the financial institution frequently finds itself bidding against trade buyers and possibly rival institutions. They often outbid trade buyers due to a willingness and ability to adopt bolder financing structures than quoted trade bidders, such as high-yield bonds and securitisation. The availability of these instruments and the relatively small equity base of IBOs enables venture capitalists to depress their cost of capital to a level where they can compete with quoted trade buyers who are anticipating synergies.

ADVANTAGES FOR MANAGEMENT OF AN MBO

What is the effect on management of this trend towards IBOs? It depends whether they see their glass as half-full or half-empty. Key advantages over an MBO for management include:

- *The ability to "pick the right horse";*

- *Sale bonuses;*

- *Involvement in larger deals.*

The MBO process is almost always nerve-racking for management. Have we picked the right venture capitalist? Will they deliver the funding? If we're sold to a trade buyer, how will they feel about our having competed against them? If the sale collapses, how will it affect our relationship with the vendor?

The IBO process mitigates these concerns and in effect allows management to wait until a winner emerges from the auction before negotiating their deal. The attraction of this approach is predicated on the reassuring fact that a venture capital investor will always seek to incentivise management.

The auction process also gives the vendor a strong motive to incentivise management: they are the salespeople that interested parties will meet at presentations and they are responsible for presenting the business in a good light and ensuring that it continues to run smoothly up to the date of disposal.

Notwithstanding directors' obligations to their employers, a means of ensuring goal congruence between vendor and management is to offer sale bonuses. These are commonly ratcheted according to the sale price, which means that management earn a bonus whoever the ultimate winner is, and if a financial institution triumphs, management have the funds to finance the purchase of their equity stake. It's also a continuing reality that the potential returns to management from a successful venture capital-backed deal outstrip anything (except, perhaps, a .com factor!) a typical senior executive share option scheme could offer.

The final advantage draws on the fundraising point discussed earlier. The increase in large funds and IBOs means that more managers can be part-equity owners in businesses that in times past would inevitably have been sold to a trade buyer, with the job insecurity and cultural issues that entails.

DISADVANTAGES FOR MANAGEMENT OF AN IBO

To a large extent the IBO's disadvantages are simply the obverse of its benefits. The two drawbacks discussed here are:

■ *Reduced influence over the process;*

■ *Smaller slice of the cake.*

The fact that vendors often seek to "rule management offside" to encourage equal treatment of all interested parties until a preferred purchaser is selected inevitably decreases management's involvement in, or excludes them from, formulation of the institution's strategy.

Management may then feel the institution is presenting them with a fait accompli and paying an unrealistic price to acquire the business. This is an acid test of pricing for the institution. If management won't invest personally, how good is the deal they've struck with the vendor? However, with good independent advice, management will usually still find scope to structure a good deal for themselves. Management are still key in these transactions – the venture capitalists will not be running the business itself and management are best placed to ensure a smooth transaction and warn the venture capitalists where any skeletons are buried. Indeed, given the workload and pressures involved, managers who've been through the MBO process may envy IBO management teams, who don't have to risk their necks to raise money and negotiate purchase of their business!

Management equity stakes, in terms of percentage shareholdings, tend to be lower in IBOs than MBOs. This is partly a product of the sheer scale of the funds involved and partly because the institution has led the transaction throughout. It is, however, important that management do not get unduly hung up about this.

First, this is because the shareholder rights contained in the subscription agreement, rather than any trigger percentages under company law, are the key determinants of control.

Second, and more importantly, even if management are offered a relatively small slice of the cake in IBOs, it's a much bigger cake than in most deals. In simple terms, managers will generally prefer 10 per cent of a £200m company to 20 per cent of a £20m one. Given the prevalence of sale bonuses, it could even be said that now they can have their cake and eat it!

CONCLUSION

Although a fairly recent development, the fashion for IBOs is not likely to go away. While it can be seen as another nail in the coffin of the cosy MBO at a bargain price, it has, at the larger end of the market, created new opportunities for managers to become equity participants in their own business. For incumbent management, the level of involvement in the early stages of striking the deal may have dropped, but the challenge of making the deal work – and the rewards for doing so – remain.

CASE STUDY

The institutional buy-out sets up hurdles all of its own, not least because of the number of different potential backers involved in negotiations.

Although Phildrew Ventures and Montagu Private Equity put up the bulk of the money for the buy-out of Dowty's electronics businesses from TI, a host of other investors included 3i, the Prudential and the Abu Dhabi Investment Authority.

The MBO was instigated by Julian Blogh, who now runs the new company Ultra Electronics. He cites the difficulty of holding the banking consortium together as his biggest headache during the buy-out process and comments: "Whatever people tell you, our sort of deal takes a lot, lot longer than you think it will."

TI was adamant at the outset that it would not sell to management, forcing Blogh to resign as managing director of Dowty Avionics. It finally relented, but obtaining exclusive negotiating rights proved another major obstacle.

The fact that both Dowty (albeit half-heartedly) and TI had previously attempted to sell the electronics businesses heaped pressure on Blogh and colleagues to achieve a swift conclusion to talks.

"We came under a lot of pressure while negotiating. TI made it clear they had potential buyers lined up for all seven of the businesses we eventually bought," says Blogh.

Unique to Ultra's MBO were the potential liabilities it faced in some defence contracts. The nature of this work is front-loaded —millions can be spent on developing bespoke defence systems for overseas governments. If these don't work or the contract is cancelled, Ultra can face a huge outlay for no return.

"The liabilities were a potential deal-breaker and took ages to negotiate with TI. But we were simply not prepared to buy the company with them, so TI agreed to retain some major risks."

Chapter 11

Buy-outs and tax

Paul Megson, tax partner of KPMG's transaction services division, outlines the tax issues that any MBO team will have to address

In designing a structure for an investment into an MBO, management and the financial institutions backing them will naturally wish to make their investments as tax efficient as practicable. They will each have their own priorities and, as with any other aspect of the transaction, these will not necessarily co-incide. So, what are their tax planning priorities likely to be?

WHAT IS MANAGEMENT LOOKING FOR?

Taxation of capital gains

First, they will be anxious to avoid an income-tax charge arising when they make their investment. This can happen if they are deemed, by reason of their employment with the target company, to have acquired or subscribed for shares on terms which differ from those on which shares are available to other investors.

If it appears that they have received their shares at an undervalue, this could be treated as taxable income and a Schedule E liability may arise, even though they have not, as yet, realised any gain.

Investments in MBOs are therefore typically structured through new companies formed specifically to acquire the target company or business. The share structures of these are designed so that management pay the same price as the equity providers, for shares which at least initially have identical rights. It is only later, at exit, that management may acquire additional rights, and then this is generally done by reducing the rights of the institutional shares rather than increasing those of the management shares.

Second, management will generally want their gains to be taxed under capital gains tax rules. Apart from a reducing liability over time with "taper relief", this permits them to mitigate their liabilities in various ways, such as gifting the shares to their children before they accrue any significant value, or transferring some shares to their spouses, so that they can shelter the gains with their own tax rates and reliefs. They might even plan to leave the UK to take their gains in a lower tax environment, although it should be noted that the Inland Revenue has recently tightened the rules governing exemption from taxation when going non-resident.

Finally, there are alternative methods of mitigating tax liabilities which do not require them to give their shares away or to emigrate. For example, if they can structure their disposal proceeds in the form of a cash or scrip dividend, they may be able to reduce the effective rate of taxation from 40 to 25 per cent.

Income tax relief on investment

In a buy-out, management are normally invited to subscribe shares for cash, rather then being granted options, to ensure that they are additionally incentivised by the prospect of a downside risk. They will want to minimise the cost of their investment with tax reliefs.

The Inland Revenue has published a series of consultation papers on new schemes to provide tax incentives for such investment, but most of these are aimed at smaller transactions or relatively small individual investments, so may turn out not to be of much interest to many management teams.

Individual investors can however obtain income tax relief for interest paid on loans taken out to finance their investments, subject to various conditions. In particular, the company must be "close" at the time that they make their investment, and it must exist for the purpose of carrying on a trade, or owning trading companies. The introduction of a financial institution as investor is likely to render any company non-close, so management must normally subscribe their shares first, before the institutions come on board. Also, if the buy-out is unsuccessful, and management fail to recover their investment, they can console themselves with income-tax relief on their capital losses, again subject to certain conditions.

WHAT ARE THE INSTITUTIONS LOOKING FOR?

Leverage

One of the key features of a typical MBO is leverage, which in tax terms means significant debt levels and high interest charges. This is particularly so when account is taken of the equity provider's preferred-return stock, which is generally structured as subordinated loan notes. To achieve this leverage, they will normally have to form a new special purpose company to make the acquisition, even where the target is a company, because they will need a vessel for the debt.

A leveraged investment will have to conform with tough financial covenants, which include covenants on profits and cashflow. If the entire interest charge, including subordinated notes and rolled-up interest, can be deducted, this can make a significant impact on net profits and free cashflow. There are however various restrictions on "thinly capitalised" companies, and on the deduction of unpaid interest. Fortunately, the limited partnership structures which many UK venture capital funds have adopted generally overcome many of these restrictions, but those which remain require careful planning to avoid.

There are no really insurmountable obstacles to tax-effective leverage in the UK, but this is not always true overseas, especially in a multinational target. In these cases it is generally essential to have tax specialists analyse the legal structure of the target group and of its vendor, to identify a transaction structure which permits debt to be pushed down into overseas locations, while not materially compromising the vendor's tax position.

Gains on exit

UK venture capital funds derive their returns predominantly from the capital gains made when the investment is sold or floated. They adopted limited partnerships, after consultation with the

Inland Revenue and the DTI, to achieve a transparency for their investors. A key consideration for fund managers is that investors should have only their own direct tax liabilities to deal with - no taxation should be imposed on the fund itself, or on any investment vehicle set up below the fund.

Investors will therefore expect to sell not the target company which they are about to acquire, but the new company which they form for the purposes of the acquisition. In rare cases where the new company itself becomes the vendor, for example where it is anticipated that assets will be sold separately before the main exit, the institutions may well be advised to use a company resident in the Netherlands, Belgium or Luxembourg to make the acquisition. This may limit the available tax deductions for interest, but no sensible investor would expose their targeted investment IRRs of 30 per cent per annum or more to taxation, for the sake of a deduction on a single-figure interest rate.

Transaction costs

The fees incurred on a typical management buy-out – bank fees around 2 per cent of the facility granted, venture capital fees typically 1 per cent of deal value, and assorted legal and professional fees – can easily add 6-8 per cent to the cost of the transaction. Institutional investors will want to get as much tax relief as possible for these.

The bank fees should be deductible without any difficulty provided that they are accounted for in accordance with the "authorised" accounting principles, typically amortising over the lives of the facilities. Some costs are simply not deductible against income in any circumstance – stamp duty for example, or fees for the actual negotiation of the purchase. There remains however a substantial area of opportunity in between where appropriate, and timely, planning can maximise tax deductions. Management and investors should be sure to instruct their tax advisers to liaise with other professionals at an early stage to structure the professional relationships in such a way as to optimise the opportunities. This is especially true of Value Added Tax.

WHAT ARE MANAGEMENT AND INVESTORS BOTH LOOKING FOR?

In practice, management have as much to gain from achieving the objectives of the investors as the investors themselves, possibly more so, if this leads to their ratchets coming into operation. More free cashflow means faster paydown of debt and a happier bank. More net profit could mean a better exit price. Both can mean better IRR for management and institutional investors alike.

However, from a tax planning perspective almost all MBOs hold traps for the unwary, or some opportunity to improve. So, always ensure that your advisers bring a tax specialist along!

Chapter 12

Exit this way

Neil Patey, corporate finance partner at Ernst & Young, guides managers through the main exit routes in the post-MBO environment

A few years after completing an MBO, managers and their backers may start looking for an exit in order to realise some, if not all, of the investment made in the business. The key question is which route to choose – flotation or trade sale?

IS FLOTATION AN OPTION?
Before MBO teams weigh up both routes, they must answer a tough question: is a flotation a viable proposition at all? Institutional investors' preference for blue chips over smaller quoted companies has been well documented in the press, and many smaller listed companies are disillusioned with the City's apparent lack of interest in them. Against this climate, most advisers would be unlikely to recommend a full London Stock Exchange flotation for a company with a potential market value below £500m without significant growth prospects.

Exceptions might include high-growth companies in sectors like IT or telecoms, which could attract institutional investor interest. Alternatively, the company's plan may be to supplement modest generic growth with bolt-on acquisitions, but the City will have to be persuaded that the strategy is viable and capable of rapid implementation.

FLOTATION PROS AND CONS
If a flotation is possible, management can choose between this option or a trade sale. Although currently unfashionable for smaller companies, flotations do provide a liquid market for shares, enabling further funds to be raised. Flotation also provides a

platform for making acquisitions, as the company can use its paper to finance future deals. A listing can raise a company's profile, which may be a valuable aid to winning contracts in highly competitive markets. Being listed also offers the company a method of incentivising employees through share schemes.

On the downside, listing is an intensive, arduous, expensive process. Costs are likely to reach £500,000 even before brokers' underwriting fees. Listing is time-consuming and puts considerable pressure on management, who must continue running the business efficiently amid flotation preparations. Once floated there are ongoing regulatory requirements to be met and time spent communicating with the City, which can be unforgiving if a business fails to meet forecasts. Some management teams become frustrated by the restrictions of operating as a quoted company.

THE UPS AND DOWNS OF TRADE SALES

A trade sale should be more straightforward than a flotation, and can be completed relatively quickly. However, negotiations may become tortuous and time-consuming. There's also a greater likelihood that the incumbent management won't be required to stay on after the sale. This can be an advantage or a disadvantage, depending on whether MBO team members want to retire or move on to new business opportunities. With a flotation, the team will have an ongoing role in running the business.

THE FLOTATION PROCESS

If flotation is the chosen option, the company will need to prove its suitability for joining the chosen exchange. All stock markets try to ensure that joining companies have suitable boards of directors, sufficiently experienced management and appropriate financial systems.

The business will also need to show healthy profit growth, so business decisions over the two years before flotation must be taken with profit impact in mind. In the final year before flotation, management has to commit significant time to preparations. The company's details, including extensive financial information, must be compiled into the listing particulars. As the listing date approaches the team will need to give presentations to brokers, sponsors and potential institutional investors. The price of shares is usually the last issue to be finalised – calculated to attract interest in all the shares yet not undervalue the company.

Throughout the process the management team will need trustworthy advisers who appreciate the company's own style, including a sponsor, a broker, a public relations company, lawyers, registrars and an accountancy firm to carry out due diligence on the listing particulars.

If management wants to float the business, it needs to choose its stock market. Most UK businesses opt to list in the UK where they have a choice between the Listed (or Main) market of the London Stock Exchange, or AIM – the Alternative Investment Market. Most investor interest is focused on the Main market, the most regulated UK market.

AIM was set up to provide capital-raising options for smaller, higher-risk companies that may not have the track record of growth required for a Full Listing. That said, potential AIM companies still need a sound business plan and the ability to attract investors.

Companies with an interest in attracting US investment, perhaps for expansion reasons, could consider joining Nasdaq in the US, which has a higher profile than AIM and has built a reputation for attracting fast-growing high-tech companies. Companies with a European-based business, potentially attractive to investors across continental Europe, could consider floating on Easdaq, a pan-European market similar to Nasdaq but newer and smaller.

HOW TO ACHIEVE A TRADE SALE

Many management teams, given current market conditions, may decide that a trade sale is more suitable for their business.

For them the process begins with the preparation of the sales document briefly describing the company, its assets, staffing and prospects, and aiming to whet potential buyers' appetites without divulging confidential commercial information. The sales memorandum should highlight the strengths of the business but remain balanced – discovery of undisclosed weaknesses will cause buyers to become suspicious, drop the offer price or withdraw.

The pool of interested parties is gradually narrowed down, while being allowed increasing but controlled access to the company, before committed bids are sought. Traditionally the vendor now chooses its preferred bidder and the two sides agree a price and enter into heads of agreement, subject to due diligence.

The vendor would then reveal all the company information to that party and the potential purchaser would call in its advisers to perform due diligence on the information, checking for flaws in the figures and undisclosed weaknesses or liabilities to negotiate the price downwards. The process can be nerve-racking for the vendor's management and puts the purchaser in a strong position.

Canny vendors often now choose to increase their control over the deal by commissioning a due diligence report themselves up-front. The report is made available to a selection of potential buyers, who base their offers on that information. This method makes it harder for the purchaser to negotiate the price downwards and the vendor can keep several potential buyers in play far longer, even until a week before completion of the deal. This approach, which has many similarities to an auction, may achieve the best price for the vendor.

THE VALUE OF ADVICE

During this process corporate finance professionals can play a valuable role in driving negotiations forward, assessing tax implications, valuing the business and advising on marketing strategies. In the final stages management and its advisers need to check the details of the deal – especially warranties, which can greatly add to or detract from the initial agreement.

When a management team seeks an exit, all possible options must be considered to achieve the best price while fulfilling management's personal objectives. Professional advisers can make sure no options are overlooked.

CASE STUDY

Venture capitalists turn down 95 per cent of the deals presented to them. The most common reasons for rejection are the unwillingness of the owner to sell or the unsuitability of the industry sector for investment.

But directors' failure to focus on the exit strategy can also prove their undoing. For Harrington Food Group this was not a problem. The directors always envisaged a trade sale, since the City's dislike of small foods companies has not changed. A piecemeal approach to the process will see Harrington broken up and sold off to several buyers over the next four to five years.

The first company, nut processor Cadec, went in December 1998. Tony Orvis comments: "As far as the City's concerned, yesterday's small company is tomorrow's minnow. There's no future in relisting.

"No single buyer is likely to want the whole group. But we agreed that it was possible to restructure over four to five years and we're now in better shape. The companies' chances of finding buyers are better now than when we were listed."

Harrington subsidiaries are all number one or two in their chosen markets. York-based dried fruits business Sundora supplies Sainsbury, Tesco and Safeway, while a processed vegetable company in Boston, Lincolnshire supplies diced product for companies such as Hazlewood Foods and Nestlé – which owns Cross & Blackwell.

Kernels Snacks Products in Yorkshire provides popcorn and has an exclusive supply deal with Virgin, ABC and Odeon cinemas.

A frozen herbs business in Suffolk, meanwhile, supplies 1,500 tons of product a year to food manufacturers. The company grows hundreds of acres of herbs under contract, something a new entrant to the market would find difficult to replicate.

"We're focused in strong niches," says Orvis. "These are good businesses with attractive revenue streams. Trade buyers will buy them individually and that's the strategy we're working to."

Chapter 13

Reasons to be cheerful

Peter Temple, a freelance financial journalist and author, highlights some success stories to encourage the faint-hearted, would-be MBO team

So, you've finally decided to mount that buy-out, or seek venture capital funding for your big idea?

You've got your business plan written – always remembering that 95 per cent of proposals fail to get backing because the plan is poorly drawn or badly presented.

You've mastered the jargon: you know your MBOs from your MBIs, your BIMBOs from your BAMBIs, and your BINGOs from your DINGOs. You knowhow to avoid needing a RAMBO, and the difference between being a "lemon" or "plum" for your backers. (Hint: lemons – deals that go bad – ripen before plums...and leave a nasty taste in the mouth!) So far so good. But is there anything else you need to bear in mind?

FORGET THE FISH...

Most private equity backers have specific pet hates that will turn them off investing in a company, however worthy it may be in other respects. These include things like directors with expensive cars (especially if they have personalised number plates), a company flagpole, or a fishtank in the boardroom.

A reception area carpet with the company logo woven into it is another definite "no-no", and some private equity backers have a distinct aversion to suede shoes, monogrammed cufflinks (or shirts), or even directors who find time to serve as JPs as well as attending to their business duties.

More seriously, what is most likely to impress is a "no-frills" approach, an efficient switchboard and motivated and enthusiastic employees. Backers typically fight shy of companies with autocratic management, evidence of poor or deteriorating credit control, dependence on a few large customers, or a high turnover of key employees.

Even if you do attract potential backers, seeing the deal through to completion can be a stressful process. One experienced buy-out veteran once described the so-called due diligence process as "like having your mother-in-law to stay for three months".

And don't forget that it's only once the deal has been concluded that the real hard work begins – persuading your customers, employees, bankers, suppliers and anyone else you might deal with that your venture has a long-term future. Not all buy-outs, and certainly not all start-ups, succeed and some of your own money will be on the line to make sure that your interests are aligned with those of your backers.

But if the risks are higher than normal, the potential rewards will be high too.

PROFITING FROM PUBS

Consider the example of Derek Mapp, the marketing director of Mansfield Brewery. He left the company to found Tom Cobleigh, harbouring a vision of launching a chain of high-quality managed pubs with a high food content. Bluff and ambitious, Mapp found his private equity alter ego in the shape of Bert Wiegman, managing director of European Acquisition Capital. EAC, now independent, was at the time a private equity fund owned by a Swedish bank.

Wiegman and Mapp got on well and EAC steadily injected funds into the start-up as it began the capital-hungry process of building up its chain of pubs. Scottish & Newcastle, one of the company's main suppliers, provided some key mezzanine finance, bridging the gap between the equity invested by EAC and what the banks were prepared to lend to the venture.

Above all Mapp's case is one where management incentives

produced a superb result for the investors in the company, and for the managers themselves. The original team put in some £300,000 of their own money. Their stake in the final "exit" was determined by a ratchet mechanism related to the internal rate of return the investment produced. As this rose above pre-set thresholds, the rewards the management team received increased sharply.

In the end the exit was a two-stage one. The company initially floated on the stock market but was subsequently taken over by the Rank Organisation for a price of £115m (including debt) in October 1996. Mapp exited from the venture with several million, but – unlike in a normal buy-out – had gained the satisfaction of creating a very substantial business, and many hundreds of jobs, from scratch. EAC's original investment of £10m in the company returned £48m in less than five years.

CASHING IN ON COMPUTING

Then there's the case of Computacenter, another private equity success story. The company, which provides IT products and services for big companies and the public sector, was founded in 1981 by Philip Hulme and Peter Ogden. They are still both large shareholders in the business they founded as their respective second careers.

Hulme and Ogden were business school alumni who met while they were at Harvard. Ogden then worked for Merrill Lynch and Morgan Stanley, while Hulme, an engineer by training, became a consultant with the Boston Consulting Group.

The founding of the business happily coincided with IBM's launch of the personal computer. In 1986 Apax Partners and F&C Ventures invested some early-stage development capital in the business in exchange for a sizeable equity stake.

F&C's stake in the business was worth some £610,000 at the time it was made, while Apax's was roughly three times that size. Immediately prior to the flotation the Apax holding was worth £266m and F&C's some £89m, an impressive multiplication of the original investment, which has also made Hulme and Ogden and many of their colleagues very rich indeed.

Computacenter's stock market value has slipped a little since its market debut, although the company continues to report impressive profits. It is currently valued (at the time of writing) at some £915m, compared with a value at flotation of £1.15bn. Hulme and Ogden still hold 24 per cent of the company each, and about thirty other members of the management team became paper millionaires as a result of the flotation.

Both of the private equity investors in the business took the opportunity of the flotation to reduce their holdings, and Apax no longer holds a disclosable stake. The deal is, however, an object lesson as to how time and patience, a good idea, and aligning the interests of management and shareholders can combine to produce sparkling return. Quite apart from the wea'th created personally by the management team, both Apax and F&C returned more than 100 times their original investment over the space of about 13 years.

FEASIBILITY, NOT FASHION

In short, if you can present yourselves well and attract backing for your bright idea, the chances are that you can create serious wealth for yourselves and your investors.

It needs to be the right idea at the right time, of course. And the backer – as well as your advisers – need to be carefully selected to mesh with your own aims and ambitions. But it doesn't necessarily have to be in a glamorous business. Often the most unprepossessing of businesses make good buy-outs if they have the right cashflow characteristics.

Above all, patience, persistence, enthusiasm and hard work can reap huge financial dividends for everyone involved.

Peter Temple is a freelance financial journalist and author. His latest book, Private Equity: Examining the New Conglomerates of European Business, *is a primer for managers seeking private equity backing and is published by John Wiley & Sons.*

AN MBO TIMETABLE

It is possible to complete an MBO within a six week timescale from initial identification of the opportunity to completion. However, this will only be achieved where all parties are keen to progress the transaction rapidly, information required is available and flows freely and the business to be acquired is relatively discreet and operates from a small number of locations. More typically, buy-outs will take between three and six months.

An MBO involves the following main steps:

- *Identify opportunity and write business plan;*

- *Management: organise, select adviser, finalise business plan;*

- *Appoint deal leader;*

- *Identify sources of finance;*

- *Agree outline terms with vendor;*

- *Conduct due diligence;*

- *Negotiate legal documentation;*

- *Completion.*

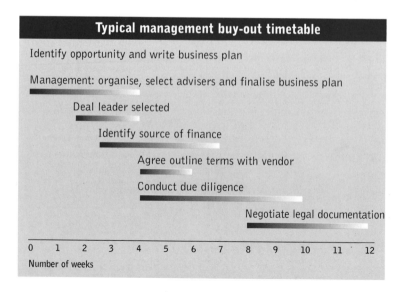

Typical management buy-out timetable

Identify opportunity and write business plan

Management: organise, select advisers and finalise business plan

Deal leader selected

Identify source of finance

Agree outline terms with vendor

Conduct due diligence

Negotiate legal documentation

| 0 | 1 | 2 | 3 | 4 | 5 | 6 | 7 | 8 | 9 | 10 | 11 | 12 |

Number of weeks